2 elephants

3 lions

4 zebras

5 hippos

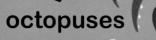

6 boats

7 octopuses

8 crabs

Which octopus is missing a leg?

Can you spot the turtle?

11
bananas

13
oranges

Which fruit is missing a slice?

14
apples

17
plums

18
strawberries

Can you spot the hungry worm?

16   17   18   19   20

12
pineapples

15
pears

16
lemons

19
limes

20
cherries

How many cherries are in each basket?

30 Hot-air balloons

Which balloon is shaped like a star?

Can you spot
the little lion?

Which balloon
has the most stripes?

40 Dinosaurs

Can you spot the
dinosaur nest?

How many dinosaurs have long necks?

Count 15 stripy dinosaurs.

50 Dogs

Can you spot a cat?

Which dog has the most spots?

How many dogs have red collars?

60 Penguins

Can you spot
the seal?

How many penguins
are on each iceberg?

Follow the fishing lines to find out which penguin is about to catch a fish.

70 Flowers

How many flower beds are there?

Follow the path to lead the duck to the pond.

Can you spot the
white rabbit?

How many cupcakes have pink cases?

Which doughnut is the odd one out?

Can you
count 16
cherries?

Can you spot
the squirrel?

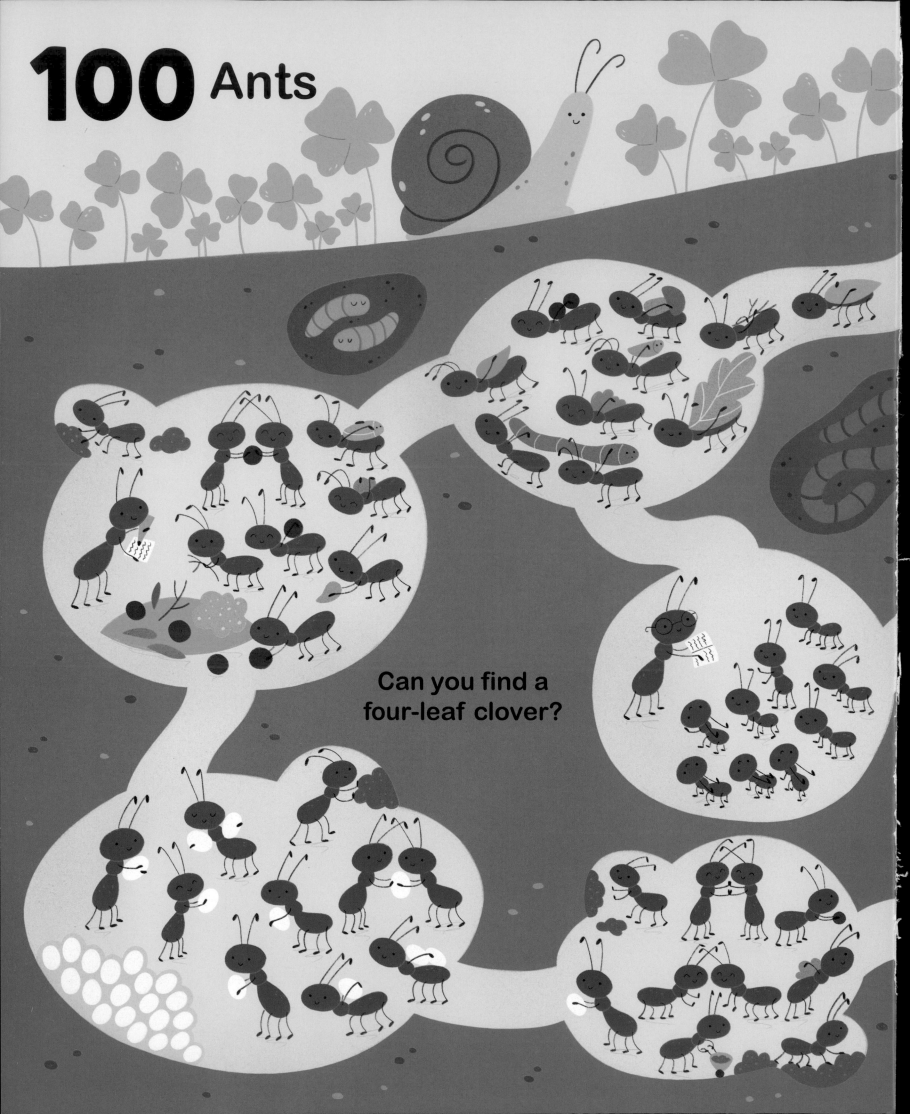

100 Ants

Can you find a
four-leaf clover?